ARFIE D

25

© PAWS

ars of me!

JIM DAVIS

RAVETTE PUBLISHING

This edition first published by Ravette Publishing 2003.
Edited by Robbie Lamb.

Printed and bound in Croatia for Ravette Publishing Limited,
Unit 3, Tristar Centre,
Star Road, Partridge Green,
West Sussex RH13 8RA

ISBN: 1 84161 173 5

In the beginning ...

1979

1979

HAPPY FIRST BIRTHDAY, GARFIELD! MAKE A WISH AND BLOW OUT THE CANDLE

6-19

FOOF!

© 1979 PAWS, INC. All Rights Reserved.

OH GEE. THAT'S TOO BAD

NOT REALLY. I GOT MY WISH

JIM DAVIS

1980

WHAT WOULD YOU LIKE FOR YOUR BIRTHDAY, GARFIELD?

ANOTHER NINE LIVES

6-16

© 1980 PAWS, INC. All Rights Reserved.

HOW ABOUT A BALL OF YARN?

HOW ABOUT NOT?

WHAT IF I KEEP YOU IN KITTY SWEATERS?

WHAT IF I KEEP YOU IN STITCHES?

JIM DAVIS

1981

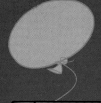

I CAN HEAR THEM SNEAKING UP BEHIND ME NOW

6-19

JiM DAViS

THEY ARE CROUCHING, GETTING READY TO LEAP

HAPPY BIRTHDAY, GARFIELD!

WHAT A WONDERFUL SURPRISE!

© 1981 PAWS, INC. All Rights Reserved.

1982

WOW. I'M GOING TO BE FOUR YEARS OLD THIS SATURDAY

JIM DAVIS

IT'S TIME TO REFLECT UPON MY ACCOMPLISHMENTS. IT'S TIME TO REMINISCE ABOUT GOOD TIMES...

6-14

IT'S TIME TO LIE ABOUT MY AGE

© 1982 PAWS, INC. All Rights Reserved.

FACE IT, GARFIELD, YOU'RE NOT GETTING ANY YOUNGER

JIM DAVIS

I WISH THERE WERE SOMETHING I COULD DO ABOUT THE AGING PROCESS

6-15

I'D DO SIT-UPS, BUT I COULDN'T STAND THE NOISE

© 1982 PAWS, INC. All Rights Reserved.

1982

1983

1984

© PAWS

1985

JIM DAVIS 6-19

SURPRISE!

© 1985 PAWS, INC. All Rights Reserved.

HAPPY BIRTHDAY, GARFIELD!

I HAD A FEELING THIS WAS COMING

1987

HEY, GARFIELD, YOU'RE GOING TO BE NINE YEARS OLD THIS FRIDAY

THANKS FOR REMINDING ME

AS CATS GO, YOU'RE APPROACHING THE GOLDEN YEARS

THE HECK WITH THE GOLDEN YEARS. I'M FIVE AND HOLDING

6-17

JIM DAVIS

1988

1988

IN A FEW DAYS I'LL BE TEN YEARS OLD. JUST WHAT **IS** TEN?

TEN IS TWO HANDS AND TWO TOES

JIM DAVIS 6-15

WHY AM I AFRAID OF TURNING TEN?

WHY AM I AFRAID TO ADMIT THAT I'M AGING?

AND WHY ARE TURKEY BUZZARDS CIRCLING MY BED?

JIM DAVIS 6-16

1989

Z

I CAN'T BELIEVE I'LL BE ELEVEN YEARS OLD TOMORROW

OH, WELL, TIME TO GET THESE OLD BONES OUT OF BED

OKAY, TOES

CRACK
CRACK CRACK
CRACK
CRACK
'CRACK

OKAY, KNEES. OKAY, ARMS

CRACK CRACK
CRACK CRACK

OKAY, KNUCKLES. OKAY, NECK

CRACK
CRACK
CRACK
CRACK
CRACK

CRACK
CRACK
CRACK
CRACK

CRACK!

ANOTHER YEAR, ANOTHER CRACK

JIM DAVIS   6-18

1989

NEXT WEEK I'M GOING TO TURN ELEVEN

GARFIELD

I WONDER IF I'LL BE OLDER AND WISER

GARFIELD

6-14

PROBABLY JUST OLDER

GARFIELD

JIM DAVIS

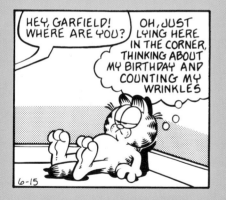
HEY, GARFIELD! WHERE ARE YOU?

OH, JUST LYING HERE IN THE CORNER, THINKING ABOUT MY BIRTHDAY AND COUNTING MY WRINKLES

6-15

THE ONLY THING THAT CAN CHEER ME UP IS TO HAVE A REALLY GREAT BIRTHDAY PARTY... WITH ALL MY BEST FRIENDS

AND *YOU'RE* NOT INVITED!

JIM DAVIS

© PAWS

1991

1992

GARFIELD

I'M A SIMPLE CAT...

I REALLY DON'T WANT MUCH FOR MY BIRTHDAY...

JUST A SIMPLE CAKE

© 1992 PAWS, INC. All Rights Reserved.

A TWO LAYER CAKE WITH STRAWBERRY ICING...

POOF

AND A CHERRY ON TOP

PING!

THAT'S ALL...

JUST A SIMPLE CAKE

JIM DAVIS 6-14

1992

SO, GARFIELD, YOU'RE GOING TO BE FOURTEEN THIS WEEK, HUH?

THANK YOU FOR REMINDING ME

FOUR-TEEN... WOW-WEE. FOURTEEN, FOURTEEN, FOURTEEN. FOUUUUUUUR-TEEEEEEN

A TEENSE SENSITIVE, ARE WE?

JIM DAVIS 6-15

A BIRTHDAY CARD! HOW NICE!

HAPPY BIRTHDAY, YOU BIG NUT. OPEN THIS CARD AND GET A...

SPLUT!

JIM DAVIS 6-18

1994

C'MON, GARFIELD, SNAP OUT OF IT. BIRTHDAYS AREN'T THAT BAD

JIM DAVIS 6-14

AFTER ALL, AGING IS ALL IN THE MIND

OF COURSE IT IS

© 1994 PAWS, INC. All Rights Reserved.

AND THE MIND IS THE FIRST THING TO GO

GARFIELD, HAVE YOU THOUGHT ABOUT WHAT YOU WANT FOR YOUR BIRTHDAY?

A GAZILLION SLAVE DOGS!

JIM DAVIS 6-16

© 1994 PAWS, INC. All Rights Reserved.

SINCE YOU'RE TURNING SIXTEEN IT SHOULD BE SOMETHING SPECIAL

WORLD DOMINATION!

HOW ABOUT A LARGE PIZZA WITH EVERYTHING?

EVEN BETTER!

1995

1995

1996

WHAT'S THE MATTER, GARFIELD?

HEY! YOUR BIRTHDAY IS NEXT WEEK!

JUNE

AND THAT'S A, UH, BAD THING, RIGHT?

JIM DAVIS 6-15

1996

YOU CAN STOP NOW

I TOLD HIM TO TAKE IT EASY 18 YEARS AGO

JIM DAVIS 6-17

1996

GARFIELD®

SO YOU'RE GOING TO BE EIGHTEEN SOON, HUH GARFIELD?

THANKS FOR THE REMINDER

I REMEMBER BACK ON THE FARM, WHEN I TURNED EIGHTEEN I REALLY CUT LOOSE

UH-HUH

MY BUDDIES AND I WENT OUT COW TIPPING

PANT PANT PANT PANT

TIP

HUH? HUH? WAS THAT FUN OR WHAT?

WHATEVER MILKS YOUR GUERNSEY

PANT PANT PANT

1996

1997

JIM DAVIS 6-16

JIM DAVIS 6-17

1998

1998

YOU LOOK DOWN, CAT

MY BIRTHDAY IS COMING UP, SCALE

JIM DAVIS 6-15
© 1998 PAWS, INC. All Rights Reserved.

HOW MANY YEARS?

TWENTY

WOW. OLD **AND** FAT

OH, GREAT...JUST WHO I **DON'T** NEED TO SEE

WHY?

JIM DAVIS 6-16
© 1998 PAWS, INC. All Rights Reserved.

IF YOU MUST KNOW, I'M HAVING A BIRTHDAY SOON

I THOUGHT IT SMELLED "OLD" IN HERE

WHERE'S NERMAL?

OUT GETTING SOME FRESH AIR

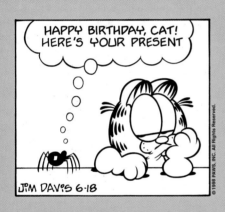

1999

1999

2001

2001

GARFIELD®

SO, BIRTHDAY NUMBER 23 IS COMING UP, EH?

YOU'RE ONLY AS YOUNG AS YOU FEEL, PAL!

SNAP!

A KITTY TREAT!

CRICK
SNAP

AND TODAY I FEEL AROUND A HUNDRED AND SIXTY-ONE

JIM DAVIS 6-17

2002

2002

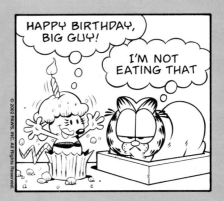

..... PARTY ON